MW01225791

Silent Night

Silent Night

A Guide to Snoring for Snorers and Their Suffering Bedmates and Families

Mark Ragg

Illustrations by Mark David

Hodder & Stoughton

A Hodder & Stoughton book

First published in Australia and New Zealand in 1996 by
Hodder Headline Australia Pty Limited
(A member of the Hodder Headline Group)
10–16 South Street, Rydalmere NSW 2116

National Library of Australia Cataloguing–in–Publication data

Ragg, Mark.
Silent night: a guide to snoring for snorers
and their suffering bedmates and families.

ISBN 0 7336 0261 4.

1. Snoring. I. Title.
612.2

Printed in Australia by Griffin Paperbacks, Adelaide

CONTENTS

Acknowledgments

The author would like to thank the following people for their help in providing material for the book, or for reading and commenting on drafts: Dr Michael Dodd, Dr Ron Grunstein, Josephine Inge, Dr Murray Johns, Christine Reddy and Professor Colin Sullivan.

Thanks also to all those friends and family members who have unwittingly supplied material for the book.

And thanks to Philippa Sandall of Hodder Headline for her enthusiasm and support.

INTRODUCTION

The night is a time of peace, of silence, of calm, of rest, of recuperation, of thought and of sleep. Or so it should be.

There are plenty of homes where the night is nothing like that. In some homes the night is a time of frustration, of worry and above all of noise. Of loud, see-sawing, annoying noise.

There is nothing new about snoring. People have laughed about it and cried about it for centuries. And you know which ones were doing the laughing — the snorers — and which ones were doing the crying — the bedmates.

Snoring has a large social cost — snorers have to sleep in the spare room and are banned from staying at friends' houses. Recently, doctors have realised that snoring is not that good for your health.

Medical interest in sleep itself is a fairly new pheno-menon, but even the first real textbook on sleep, which was published in 1963, devoted only 22 lines to snoring among its 370 pages.

Now, medical journals have gone past debating whether snoring can do harm, and they debate how much harm snoring can do. Is it only a problem for a few snorers who suffer from a condition known as obstructive sleep apnoea? Or is everyone who snores affected?

Silent Night takes up that interest and pushes it from debate among doctors to information for the people who really need it — the snorers and their suffering mates. It has information about how we breathe, how we sleep and why we (or some of us) snore.

You'll find answers to a few of your questions about snoring, and information on what can be done about snoring and where to get help.

If you're a snorer, you'll also find out how other people see you. And if you live with a snorer, you'll find some useful ammunition.

Sweet dreams.

WHAT IS SNORING?

NORMAL BREATHING

Breathing is so easy, we can do it in our sleep. Well, it looks easy, but it does take quite a bit of coordination from nerves and muscles that act subconsciously to make it all happen. Here's a list of all the parts of the airway that play a part, and a description of the part they play.

Mouth Ideally, the mouth shouldn't be used for breathing, but many people use it that way. The roof of the mouth is the palate.

Palate The front of the roof of the mouth is the hard palate, which is made of bone. Its main role, apart from separating the mouth and nose, is to provide an echo chamber for noise so we can speak. Also, we press our tongues against the hard palate to make sounds such as 'd', 'j', 'n' and 't'.

The back of the roof of the mouth is a layer of muscle known as the soft palate. The soft palate's main role is to separate the nose from the mouth, which stops your cup of tea coming out your nose when you swallow. It also helps the quality of your speech.

Nose This is what you *should* use to breathe. The nose contains hair to filter dust and other particles, and it warms the air as it passes through.

Pharynx The pharynx is the area at the back of the mouth. Air coming through the nose or mouth passes into the pharynx then on down into the trachea. The pharynx also contains the tonsils and the uvula.

Uvula The uvula is the dangly thing at the back of your mouth. It's main role seems to be to wobble wildly in cartoon characters to show they are singing loudly. If it does something useful, it hasn't told anybody about it.

Tonsils The tonsils are really lymph glands in the back of your mouth. They collect bacteria, viruses and other bits of junk and neutralise them.

They are protected, in a way, by flaps of tissue that stretch from the top of the mouth to the bottom. Those flaps are known as the posterior faucial pillars of the tonsils or, less formally, as the tonsillar flaps.

Adenoids The adenoids are similar in many ways to the tonsils, being small lymph glands. They sit a little higher than the tonsils, more towards the back of the nose.

The main thing adenoids seem to do is swell up, especially in children. The end result is ear infections, if they block the Eustachian tube running between the throat and the ear, and a nasal voice. After that, the only other thing they do is get chopped out by surgeons.

Trachea The trachea is the windpipe — a long pipe with firm cartilage rings around it to hold it stiff. It is the conduit for air from the pharynx to the lungs.

Epiglottis A small flap which separates the trachea from the pharynx, and stops food and drink getting into your lungs.

Lungs The lungs are large collections of air-containing sacs, with airways called bronchi to connect those sacs to the trachea. The lungs contain many tiny blood vessels. Oxygen passes from the lungs into the blood and carbon dioxide passes from the blood into the lungs. In that way, you breathe in oxygen and breathe out carbon dioxide.

Diaphragm The diaphragm is a strong muscular and fibrous band separating the chest from the abdomen. When the diaphragm contracts, the lungs are pulled down and expanded. This reduces the air pressure in the lungs, and air rushes in through the nose and/or mouth to equalise the pressure. Without even knowing it, you're breathing.

Chest wall You have lots of small muscles between your ribs. At the same time as your diaphragm contracts, many of these small muscles contract. This lifts the ribs up and out, again expanding the lungs and allowing air to rush in.

The airways: from nostrils to lungs

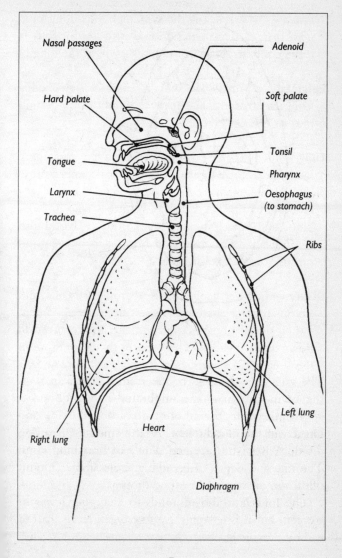

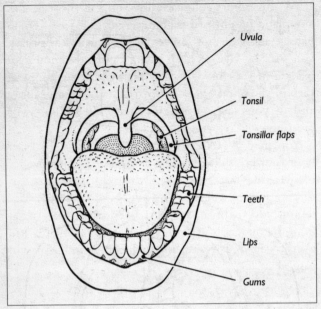

A wide open mouth

The trigger to breathe comes from a central part of the brain known as the midbrain. The midbrain is very sensitive to the amount of carbon dioxide and oxygen in the bloodstream. As the amount of carbon dioxide rises, the rate and depth of breathing rises. The rate and depth of breathing drops if the amount of carbon dioxide in the blood drops.

The midbrain also responds to changing levels of oxygen, but it is less sensitive to oxygen levels than to carbon dioxide levels.

All this occurs automatically. You can override this automatic system of breathing regulation to a certain extent, although not forever. If you breathe very fast, you may be able to keep going until the amount of oxygen in your blood is very high and the amount of carbon dioxide is very low. You will become dizzy and, if you keep going, may pass out. Then your breathing will return to normal.

You may be able to breathe very slowly, or even hold your breath, for quite a long period. The level of oxygen in your blood will drop and the level of carbon dioxide will rise. The midbrain will respond by telling you to breathe faster. Eventually, that signal from the midbrain will become so powerful that it will overpower your desire not to breathe, and you will gasp in air.

A one-year-old boy was admitted to a hospital in Paris because he had trouble feeding and was not putting on weight. His tonsils were huge, he had an enlarged uvula and his heart was racing. Tests showed he often stopped breathing while asleep, so doctors took out his tonsils and adenoids. Immediately, he started sleeping better. Within a week his heart had slowed down. Within a month he was putting on weight.

The doctors believe the obstruction to his breathing was slowing down his entire body. Allowing him to breathe more easily allowed him to sleep and feed more easily.

NORMAL SLEEP

"Sleep is a reversible behavioural state of perceptual disengagement from and unresponsiveness to the environment". Well, that's the catchy way one medical textbook defines it. The way most of us would describe sleep is to say that sleep is what you do when you're not awake.

Researchers have divided sleep into separate stages. The most important distinction is between REM sleep and non–REM sleep.

REM sleep

REM sleep stands for rapid eye movement sleep. REM sleep occurs for short periods four to six times a night. Your body is absolutely still, but your eyes are moving rapidly. You are probably dreaming while in REM sleep. Your brain is more active than when you are awake. Many men have erections during REM sleep, even more than at other times.

REM sleep is absolutely essential for a good night's sleep. People who don't have good REM sleep just don't feel refreshed, no matter how long they sleep.

Non-REM sleep

Non-REM sleep is all the rest. You don't dream as much as in REM sleep, although you may be moving around and twitching.

Non-REM sleep has four stages. Stage 1 is shallow sleep, from which it is very easy to wake. Stage 4 is very deep sleep, and if you wake while in stage 4 sleep you may feel quite groggy and confused. The others lie between.

The sleep cycle

The usual pattern of healthy sleep goes like this. You fall asleep gradually, getting into a deeper and deeper sleep, passing through stages, 1, 2, 3 and 4. After about 80 minutes, you enter your first stage of REM sleep. That REM sleep is quite brief — often less than five minutes.

You then head towards stage 1 sleep, and may even wake briefly. Then you head back down towards REM sleep, passing through stages 2, 3 and 4 on the way.

In general, episodes of REM sleep occur about 90 minutes apart. REM sleep can last as little as five minutes, or as long as an hour or more. It takes up a larger part of sleep as the night goes on.

Breathing during sleep

When you are asleep, your breathing changes slightly from when you are awake. For one thing, all your muscles relax, meaning that the muscles around the pharynx become floppy. Also, the midbrain becomes less sensitive than normal to the amount of oxygen and carbon dioxide in the bloodstream.

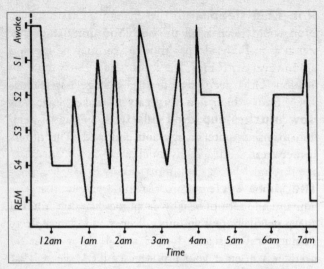

Stages in a typical night's sleep

So while you are in non-REM sleep, you are breathing slightly more slowly and slightly less deeply than while awake. In REM sleep, you may be breathing faster than normal, although you are still less rousable.

All of that means that if there is an obstruction to breathing, you respond more slowly while asleep than you normally would while awake.

The heart in sleep

While you are asleep, you are not moving around as much and many of your organs are slowing down. This means your cells don't need as much oxygen as during the day, so the flow of blood can slow.

The heart responds to the changing circumstance by slowing down a little. The blood pressure drops, too.

However in REM sleep, your heart may race at times.

How much sleep do I need?

It's a common enough question, but there is no good answer to it. You need as much sleep as you need to get through the day without feeling tired, sleepy or having poor concentration. For some people, that's 10 hours, while for others it's four or five.

We need different amounts of sleep at different ages. There is a general rule that as a child grows older, it needs less sleep. The exception is puberty — at that time of tremendous growth, many adolescents temporarily increase their need for sleep. But otherwise, the desire for and need for sleep reduces gradually throughout life.

Figures have been collated on the average amount of sleep we get at different ages. These figures don't show us what we need, they show us what we get.

yawn

"Here, indeed, was his [US president Calvin Coolidge's] one ... really notable talent. He slept more than any other president, whether by day or by night. Nero fiddled, but Coolidge only snored."

HL Mencken in *American Mercury*, April 1933.

Age	Average sleep (hours)
1 week	16.5
1 month	15.5
3 months	15
6 months	14.25
1 year	13.75
2 years	13
5 years	11
10 years	9.75
16 years	8.5

By adult life, we settle down to getting 7 to 7.5 hours a night on average.

If a child is functioning normally during the daytime — is not sleepy and seems as well behaved as you could expect a child to be — then he or she is having enough sleep. But if the child seems irritable and sleepy, gets exhausted in the hour or two before bedtime, or dozes off while sitting still or watching TV, then more sleep may be needed. The same with adults.

HOW MUCH SLEEP?

Albert Einstein slept less than four hours a night, and that gave him plenty of time to think. Margaret Thatcher boasted that she needed only four hours sleep a night, but she always acted like she needed more.

WHAT IS SNORING?

Snoring is an annoying noise that everybody makes at some time, some people make at most times, a few people make all the time, and everybody denies making.

It is caused mainly by vibration of the soft palate and the tonsillar flaps. In some people, the whole pharynx almost collapses in.

When snorers breathe in, the soft palate and the tonsillar flaps flutter in the breeze, making a noise. Sometimes, in really heavy snorers, you get the noise on the way out, too.

In general, snoring becomes louder as your level of sleep increases. But when you get to REM sleep, the snoring usually eases slightly.

IMITATION SNORING

Try to pretend you're snoring. Make that sound. Now notice what you did. You lifted the back of your tongue up and back until it touched your soft palate. The sides of your pharynx also moved in. The noise was made by all those pieces of tissue bouncing together and apart, together and apart.

When you breathed out, you let your tongue, pharynx and palate relax and the air flowed out noisily, but easily. It did not have the noise of that vibration. That, too, is what happens in snoring.

Who snores?

It is not all that common for babies and children to snore, although some do. The incidence of snoring increases in men after the age of twenty, and in women after the age of forty. By the age of sixty, about 50 per cent of men and 40 per cent of women snore most nights.

Overall, about 25 per cent of us snore most nights, and a further 20 per cent snore some nights. Fat people are three times more likely to snore than thin people.

These figures may not be all that accurate, because it is quite hard to tell whether people snore or not. If you ask a random sample of men, you will get one figure. If you ask their partners too, that figure doubles. Some men either don't know, or won't admit it.

SNORING AND OBSTRUCTIVE SLEEP APNOEA

The term "obstructive sleep apnoea" was coined by French-American sleep scientist Christian Guille-minault in the early 1970s.

Apnoea is a word which means "no breathing". Sleep apnoea is a syndrome in which you stop breathing for short periods — 10 seconds or longer — repeatedly through the night. Obstructive sleep apnoea is the particular form of sleep apnoea caused by a narrowing and regular blockage of the upper airways. The other form of sleep apnoea is central sleep apnoea, in which the cause of the apnoea lies in the brain, not the pharynx.

Obstructive sleep apnoea is not the same as snoring. If you snore, parts of your airway vibrate and make a noise. If you have obstructive sleep apnoea, your airways collapse temporarily but frequently, and no fresh air gets into your lungs.

Only a proportion of people who snore have obstructive sleep apnoea and, oddly, it is possible to have obstructive sleep apnoea without snoring. The two are closely linked, though. Most people who develop obstructive sleep apnoea have snored for years beforehand. In a way, sleep apnoea is what happens if you carry snoring to excess.

To recognise this fact, some doctors are trying to ditch the term "obstructive sleep apnoea" and replace it with "heavy snorers' disease", which would incorporate people who snore without totally blocking off their pharynx. They believe that snoring by itself is enough of a health hazard to warrant this, although this is a controversial area.

Obstructive sleep apnoea was first recognised as a problem in the late 1960s, although knowledge of it has been fairly slow to spread. Some doctors still don't consider the study of sleep and its disorders as a "real" branch of medicine, and that attitude has inhibited the ability of doctors to get funds for research. It also means that some doctors have little interest in sleep, and some may even dismiss questions about snoring as if they are not worth bothering about.

Still, the knowledge of sleep problems is spreading. Many more people now than 10 years ago take sleep

A British doctor was seeing two patients with an unusual problem — they had severe ulcers on their tongues. When the doctor probed a little deeper, it turned out that both snored heavily, both were exhausted in the morning and both were sleepy during the daytime.

The doctor realised that both had obstructive sleep apnoea. Both people were making such violent attempts to breathe after their apnoeic episode that they were biting their tongues. Treatment for the sleep apnoea helped their ulcers get better.

---

seriously and accept that snoring can be a sign of potentially serious problems.

But there is a lot to learn. Doctors know a fair bit about sleep apnoea, although they are still not sure of the extent to which it causes some diseases. And they are not sure how badly snoring without apnoea affects your health — some believe it is irrelevant while others believe it is quite significant. However, there is no doubt that if snoring is a part of sleep apnoea, it is a sign of problems.

There is still plenty of research needed into snoring and sleep apnoea. By the time a second edition of this book is printed, we should have more answers.

SECTION TWO

QUESTIONS AND ANSWERS

WHY DO MORE MEN THAN WOMEN SNORE?

One reason men are more likely to snore than women arises from the way men and women carry their weight. When men put on weight, it goes on the trunk. Men get fat necks, fat chests and fat bellies. The stereotypical fat man has the beer belly with little stick legs poking out from underneath.

Women put on weight elsewhere. Women get big bums, big hips, large breasts and fat arms and legs. They tend not to get as fat in the neck, and certainly not as fat in the belly.

It seems that the central distribution of fat in men plays a part, while women's peripheral distribution of fat somehow protects them (see page 24, Why do fat people snore?).

"Old women snore violently. They are like bodies into which bizarre animals have crept at night: the animals are vicious, bawdy, noisy. How they snore! There is no shame to their snoring. Old women turn into old men."

Joyce Carol Oates in "What is the connection between men and women?" *Mademoiselle*, February 1970.

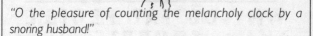

"O the pleasure of counting the melancholy clock by a snoring husband!"

George Farquhar in *The Beaux' Strategem*, Act II

But not that's not the only reason. Men drink more alcohol most days and get drunk more often, so that relaxes their pharyngeal muscles more. Older men are more likely to smoke than younger men, and that makes them snore. As well, men sleep with their mouth open more often than women, although it is not clear whether this is a cause of sleep apnoea or an effect of it.

There may be something else important. Some women start snoring after menopause, which makes you wonder whether the hormones oestrogen or progesterone somehow protect them from snoring. Progesterone stimulates breathing, so it may somehow protect women from snoring.

Researchers at Sydney University tried to test out this idea by giving hormone replacement therapy (HRT) to women with obstructive sleep apnoea after menopause. The dose they used had no effect on their snoring, although they were heartened by a very slight reduction in the number of apnoeic episodes. They think that maybe treatment for longer periods or using a higher dose of HRT will make a difference.

WHY DO FAT PEOPLE SNORE?

F at people don't just have more fat in their arms, legs and trunk, they have more fat all over. This means they also have more fat around their pharynx, which tends to narrow the airway. A narrow airway is easier to collapse, so it is more likely that fat people will snore. Experts in sleep disorders reckon they can walk down the street and pick who will snore by the size of their necks.

But it's not just that. Even men of average weight who snore have thicker waists than men of average weight who don't snore. In fact, you can predict who will snore more easily by examining a man's waist

A 60-year-old obese woman couldn't stay awake during the day. She snored so badly she often went blue, and she was quite ill with high blood pressure, swollen legs and diabetes. She was admitted to hospital, and a CAT scan showed she had a tumour on her adrenal gland. This tumour caused her to produce too many steroids, which upset the balance of sodium, potassium and fluid in her body. Apart from making her ill, this imbalance made her tendency to snoring and sleep apnoea much worse than it should have been. When she was treated for her tumour, the snoring and sleep apnoea eased up.

measurement than his neck measurement. It seems to come down to the fact that something to do with the amount of fat in the body makes you snore. Some of it is the physical weight of the fat pushing in on the throat, but something else is at play.

The first step towards fixing snoring for most people is to lose weight. Sometimes, just losing 5kg can make a difference.

WHY DOES LYING ON YOUR BACK MAKE YOU SNORE?

The world is divided into those who snore, and those who don't. Non-snorers who lie on their backs have little change in their pharynxes. But when snorers lie back, their pharynx becomes very floppy and the resistance to airflow increases dramatically.

One research group has actually measured the area available for airflow at a certain point of the pharynx while people were in different positions.

While sitting, the average cross-sectional area of the pharynx was 1.65cm^2, but it dropped to 1.36cm^2 when the subjects lay down. There was no difference between lying on their back and lying on their side. The reason you are more likely to snore while flat on your back lies with gravity — when on your back, your tongue falls backwards to partially obstruct your pharynx.

There is one way to increase the size of your airway, making snoring less likely. Lying with your neck extended — with your chin up and head back —increases the average cross-sectional area in the pharynx to 1.94cm^2.

WHY DOES DRINKING MAKE YOU SNORE?

We all know that alcohol relaxes the muscles. It doesn't just relax the muscles of the legs, making you want to lie down, or those of the brain, making you sound like an idiot when you try to elucidate your theories on the meaning of life while tanked, but it also relaxes the muscles of the pharynx.

This means that when you breathe, the walls of the pharynx fall in a little more than they normally would. That sets up the whole scenario of vibrating pharynx and wobbling uvula, and makes men who have had a drink or three snore. The more relaxed they are, the louder they snore. So the partner doesn't just get a drunk in bed next to them, they get a loud drunk.

There is something else about drinking that makes any problems caused by snoring worse. That is that excessive drinking causes brain damage, and that may include damage to the midbrain (see page 8). If the

"He drank the Night away Till rising Dawn, then snor'd out all the Day."

Horace's *Satires* book I, chapter iii. Written in the first century BC.

midbrain is damaged, your brain may not respond as quickly as it should to a lack of oxygen. Long periods with low levels of oxygen may cause heart problems, further brain damage and harm to other organs.

One more factor may be important. Alcohol makes the blood vessels of the skin and the lining of the mouth, nose and pharynx dilate. So the lining swells slightly, which may worsen any pre-existing obstruction. The snoring gets louder.

WHY DOES SMOKING MAKE ME SNORE?

People who smoke at all are twice as likely to snore as those who don't. People who smoke 40 a day are 40 times more likely to have severe sleep disturbances than those who don't smoke.

Smoking probably causes snoring because of its irritant effect. Cigarette smoke is a fairly nasty thing to have running up and down your airways, and your airways don't like it at all. They become inflamed, swell up and produce mucus.

That swelling narrows the airways, making someone who is predisposed to snoring more likely to do so.

If you give up smoking, the lining of your airways settles down fairly soon. Within a few weeks, most of the swelling and inflammation has disappeared, although you will still have mucus deep in your lungs for a while. But the likelihood of you snoring should return to normal within a few weeks.

Apart from the direct effect of smoking, it also affects all those things that snoring does to you. Snoring can damage your heart — so does smoking. Snoring might raise your blood pressure — so does smoking. Snoring increases your risk of having a stroke — so does smoking.

So snoring and smoking double your risk of these things going wrong.

COULD MY NOSE BE MAKING ME SNORE?

Thin people snore, too. Young people snore, too. It's not just the oldies and the fatties who do it.

If you have narrowed airways in your nose, then three things happen. The first is that you are more likely to breathe through your mouth than other people, and mouth-breathers are big snorers. The second thing is that because your nasal passages are narrower, the air tends to rush through faster than if the passage was wide. Faster-flowing air produces more flutter of the palate and uvula and everything else, so it means you are more likely to snore, and any snoring you do is likely to be loud. The third is that if you have a narrow nose, the other parts of your airway may also be narrow. So what is it about the nose?

Some people have what is known as a deviated nasal septum. The thin piece of cartilage and bone that separate the two halves of the nose might be crooked (whether from birth or from a broken nose), and that can make breathing through the nose difficult.

Some people have noses that block off regularly, such as those with nasal polyps or allergies which make their nose run. And some people just have long thin noses with narrow airways.

COULD IT BE THE SHAPE OF MY FACE?

Several years ago doctors at the San Raffaele Hospital in Milan measured the dimensions of the facial bones in a group of people who didn't snore, in a group who did snore but were otherwise OK and in a group who snored and had obstructive sleep apnoea.

They found that some of the snorers had narrower jaws than average, and that the base of their skulls was narrower, too. They felt that this predisposed them to snoring.

How? To make sense, it must be that different shapes of faces encourage different patterns of airflow within the nose, mouth and pharynx. This would lead to a different likelihood of snoring.

WHAT HAS SNORING GOT TO DO WITH BLOOD PRESSURE?

Maybe a lot, maybe nothing. The two certainly go together. Many men who are overweight have high blood pressure. Many men who smoke have high blood pressure. Snoring is more common in men who are fat and who smoke. So does snoring cause high blood pressure? Or do the two just go together in the same group of people?

There are some doctors who argue that snoring causes high blood pressure. Somehow, the effort of breathing while asleep and the low levels of oxygen in

Sleep apnoea can even mimic heart problems. Three people had been investigated repeatedly for suspected heart problems, although nothing substantial had been found. They used to wake at night with palpitations and pains in their chest, feeling short of breath. It wasn't until doctors at the Mayo Clinic in the United States really got them to explain their problems that they suspected sleep apnoea. They tested them, and found these people were stopping breathing, on average, once a minute throughout the night. The amount of oxygen in their blood dropped to less than half of what it should have been. All this was putting enormous stress on their heart and causing the pains and palpitations.

the blood at night combine to raise the blood pressure. In most people, blood pressure falls slightly at night. But not in snorers.

Then there are others who say it is just coincidence that the two occur together. Well, not coincidence, but not cause and effect. It operates in the same way as some 50-year-old men getting red MGs, and also developing a hankering after young blonde women. The phallic symbol of a car does not cause the trophy bride to appear, but the same yearning for youth that drives a man to chase one also drives him to chase the other.

In this way, whatever factors cause a man to snore (obesity, smoking, alcohol) also cause his high blood pressure.

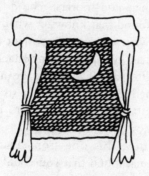

CAN SNORING REALLY GIVE ME A STROKE?

Yes, yes, undoubtedly yes. A number of studies in the past few years have shown that regular snorers are more likely to have strokes than non-snorers.

In one study of older people in Newcastle in the north of England, the most significant factor for having a stroke, or indeed for dying at all, was snoring. Snorers died sooner than non-snorers. Snorers had more strokes than non-snorers. The doctors carrying out the study found that knowing whether somebody snored or not was even more important than knowing whether they had ever had a heart attack in trying to predict their lifespan. That same group found that people who had already suffered a stroke and who snored in hospital were more likely to die within six months than those who didn't snore.

Another study, this one from Tianjin Medical College in China, found that you could better predict someone's chance of having a stroke by knowing

whether they snored or not than by knowing whether they smoked, had heart disease or had strokes in the family.

How does snoring cause strokes? It is likely that the vibration of the snoring rattles your aorta and the arteries in your neck. This shakes off tiny pieces of atheroma, which is the build-up of cholesterol and other muck lining your arteries. If a large enough piece breaks off and lodges in your brain, you have a stroke.

CAN SNORING REALLY DAMAGE MY HEART?

If you snore heavily and have sleep apnoea, there is no doubt your heart is being damaged. During that period when you stop breathing, the level of oxygen drops, your heart rate drops, you pump less blood out and your blood pressure rises. When you stir and start breathing again, your heart races and your blood pressure rises even further, sometimes to dangerously high levels. Then all returns to normal before the cycle starts again.

One study found that the heart actually stopped for short periods (two to 13 seconds) in about 10 per cent of people with obstructive sleep apnoea. In another

A 71-year-old Japanese man was known to snore very loudly at night, and often dozed off during the day. One time he was sitting in his chair, having a nap and snoring loudly, when his heart stopped. Fortunately, he was resuscitated.

While most snorers who die of heart disease were usually known to have those problems, this man was different. He wasn't fat, he didn't smoke, his blood pressure was normal and his heart, as far as any tests could show, was absolutely normal.

This case highlights the pressure that snoring puts on your heart.

7 per cent, the rate dropped to below 30 beats per minute, which is highly dangerous. Other abnormalities of the heart rate and rhythm were found in a further 7 per cent of the group.

Another small recent study has found that sleep apnoea is commonly found in men who suffer at night with severe angina, which is pain in the chest caused by heart disease.

Although there is quite a bit of dispute about whether people with sleep apnoea have an increased risk of having a heart attack, the most common feeling is that the connection exists. In fact, some doctors are so convinced of the link that they recommend people waiting for a heart transplant be screened for sleep apnoea. They feel it should be dealt with before any operation takes place, as they don't want to put extra stress on a new heart.

CAN SNORING REALLY GIVE ME BRAIN DAMAGE?

Nobody is too sure about that. It is well known that people with sleep apnoea have poor concentration and poor memory. They do quite badly on formal psychological testing.

Is this because they are so tired from never getting a good night's sleep that they can't function properly during the day?

Or it is because the episodes of low oxygen in their blood have given them repeated episodes of minor brain damage?

The answer is not clear. Most doctors working in the area probably favour the first explanation, but more research is needed before we know for sure.

A 50-year-old Japanese man with the rare problem of the neuro-Behcet syndrome was demented, could barely stand straight and snored loudly. An MRI, which is a flash version of the CAT scan, showed swelling in one part of the man's brainstem and wasting in another part. The brain damage was making him snore.

CAN SNORING AFFECT MY HORMONES?

It is not clear why, but people with obstructive sleep apnoea have abnormalities in the hormones.

Firstly, they may produce too little testosterone, although it is not clear what effect this has.

The second problem is that they may produce too little growth hormone, which comes from the pituitary gland at the base of the brain. This probably occurs because growth hormone is produced at night, so disturbed sleep will cause poor growth hormone production. If you have too little growth hormone, you tend to become fat and lose bulk from your muscles and bones. To close the circle, the fatness makes it more likely you will suffer from sleep apnoea.

It has often been seen that children with chronically enlarged tonsils and/or adenoids who have them removed suddenly start growing.

Maybe the tonsils have been causing obstruction, which has led to a deficiency in growth hormone production, which has caused the child to grow too slowly. Remove the tonsils, the growth hormone production returns to normal and the kid shoots up.

Maybe that's what happens. Or maybe not. It's only a theory at this stage.

WHY DO I WAKE UP
WITH HEADACHES?

Many people who snore wake up with a headache, and there are two main reasons.

The first is that if the airflow into your lungs is obstructed and you're not breathing as you should, you will not be getting rid of the carbon dioxide from your blood as efficiently as you should. When carbon dioxide builds up, the blood vessels in your head dilate. This gives you the feeling that your head is pounding.

The second reason is that, quite simply, some people who snore wake up feeling that they haven't had enough sleep. They have the headache of tiredness.

WHY DO I SWEAT AT NIGHT?

For the same reason that some people wake up with headaches, some snorers sweat heavily at night.

The excessive carbon dioxide causes dilatation of not just the blood vessels in your head, but the blood vessels throughout the body. More blood flows to the skin and the skin temperature rises.

As a result of that, you pour out sweat to try to lower the skin temperature. After all, that is what sweating is for.

As well, the low levels of oxygen in the blood of snorers makes them sweat.

DOES SNORING CAUSE NERVE DAMAGE?

Yes, it probably can. It has been shown that people with obstructive sleep apnoea can't detect hot and cold in their mouths as well as normal people can. This probably means the mouths and pharynxes of snorers are slowly damaged by all that vibration. The nerves running to the lining of the mouth and pharynx are repeatedly stretched and relaxed, stretched and relaxed, stretched and relaxed. Eventually, they become damaged.

It is just possible that because the nerves are damaged, the reflexes that allow the pharynx to adjust quickly to different conditions are damaged. This might allow the pharynx to flop in and may induce obstructive sleep apnoea.

There is another way nerves can be damaged. One survey has found that loud snorers have worse hearing than the average person of their age. It is just possible that the loud snoring each night is damaging their own hearing.

CAN SNORING GIVE ME NIGHTMARES?

Doctors are not too sure about this. Some studies have shown that people who snore are more likely than the norm to have nightmares, but others have not.

If snoring *does* cause nightmares, it is probably because the snoring leads to a drop in the amount of oxygen in the blood, and this leads to a disorder in the usual way the brain works. But the problem with this theory is that it is suggesting that nightmares is a sign of disordered brain function. And there is no evidence of that.

Another explanation is that snoring doesn't give you nightmares at all. Instead, people who snore wake more often, so they are more likely to remember some of their dreams and nightmares.

WHY CAN'T I SLEEP
IF I'M SNORING?

This is an odd one, but some people snore so much that they hardly feel they are getting any sleep. In fact, the need for 10 to 12 hours sleep is one of the features of severe sleep apnoea. It goes like this.

You snore heavily and your pharynx closes over. The amount of oxygen in your blood drops. You feel a choking sensation and wake, taking a few deep breaths to get things going again. As soon as you drop off to sleep, it happens again.

In the end, you are waking so often that you feel like you are not even getting to sleep. So you either get up feeling horrible for lack of sleep, or you sleep through the alarm in an attempt to catch up. Either way, it's not healthy.

WHY DOES SNORING
GIVE ME HEARTBURN?

When your airways get partially or completely blocked off, as they do with snoring, the muscles in your stomach and oesophagus relax. This allows acid from the stomach to flow back up into the oesophagus, giving that familiar burning sensation.

If you are having reflux in bed at night but at no other times, snoring could be a cause.

WHY DO I NEED TO GET UP TO GO TO THE TOILET SO OFTEN?

Normally, you don't make much urine at night. For reasons thought to be due to our natural circadian rhythm, your kidneys produce less urine at night than during the day. This is fortunate, because the bladder has a limited capacity, and if you didn't slow down, then you'd be up to the toilet all night.

If your snoring is severe enough to disturb your sleep, you never get right into the relaxed deep sleep your body needs. If you don't get that deep sleep, your body clock does not properly realise that it is night time. So your hormones don't turn down the production of urine, and your kidneys keep working as if it is daytime. You produce the regular daylight amounts of urine, so you have to get up more often to go.

Another factor which must come into to it is that snorers sleep more lightly than non-snorers. So if your bladder is full, you are more likely to realise it and get up than someone who is sound asleep.

CAN SNORING CLOUD MY THINKING?

There is fairly good evidence that people who snore every night have poor memory and concentration. This link is even stronger in people with obstructive sleep apnoea.

The researchers who have made this link believe it is indirect. They think that people who snore regularly sleep badly, which makes them sleep during the day and impairs their concentration. That impairs their memory.

Another explanation is that a lot of the work to lay down memory in the brain takes place at night. A disturbed night's sleep will interfere with the storage of memory. And with a poor memory, concentration is difficult.

IS MY SNORING
MAKING ME SLEEPY?

There's a fair chance that if you are sleepy during the day and tend to doze off easily, your snoring may have something to do with it. You might fall asleep waiting at the traffic lights, or during boring meetings. In severe cases, some people even fall asleep at the dinner table or in the middle of conversations.

People who snore toss and turn a lot and wake quite a bit during the night, even if they don't remember it. Also, their sleep is not as deep and refreshing as that of non-snorers. There is less REM sleep. So snoring might be making you drowsy. In the case of people who have obstructive sleep apnoea, the snoring is almost certainly the cause of their sleepiness.

But it doesn't have to be snoring. There are a million other reasons for being sleepy during the day. You might be a shiftworker, so your body clock is all out of whack. You might be anaemic or depressed, and the tiredness that goes with both those conditions makes you drowsy. You might be using drugs or alcohol which upset your sleep at night and alertness during the day.

Or you might have children. You might have pre-school children who, like mine, sleep soundly between 7pm and 11pm then, when their parents are jus dozing off, decide it's time to party.

You might have newborn babies who want to be fed and cuddled and changed and cuddled, then fed again within three hours.

You might have teenagers who don't feel the need to get home until 3am, which means you can't sleep until 4am because you've lain there waiting to hear they are safe, then you have to wait for an hour until your anger at their lack of consideration in getting home safely and making all worry unnecessary dies down.

If you are drowsy during the day, snoring could be the cause. But you have to look at the rest of your life, too.

IS IT SAFE TO
SNORE AND DRIVE?

No, it is not. Snoring makes some people so drowsy that they are unable to stay awake. Researchers have shown that people with obstructive sleep apnoea have more car accidents, work accidents and sick days than non-snorers.

In one piece of research, 15 people with sleep apnoea were asked to sit behind the wheel of a simulated driving test for 60 to 90 minutes. All together they ran off the road 101 times, which is an average of more than six times each. In comparison, 15 people who did not snore ran off the road a total of twice.

In one case in Britain, a transport driver with severe sleep apnoea ran off the road into a line of stationary cars, killing six people. He was sentenced to three years in prison.

If you snore heavily and regularly, and feel drowsy during the day, you should think carefully about whether you can concentrate well enough to drive, and about whether you can guarantee that you will stay awake while driving.

CAN DRUGS MAKE YOU SNORE?

Yes, drugs can make you snore. If you take sleeping pills, sedatives or antihistamines, these will all make you drowsy. They will also relax the muscles around your pharynx, making it more likely to flop about in the breeze.

Some people get themselves caught into a vicious cycle. They are having trouble breathing at night, so they have trouble sleeping. They have trouble sleeping at night, so they're tired next day. To fix the problem, they take sleeping tablets.

The sleeping tablets relax the muscles in their pharynx even more, and the obstruction that is interrupting their sleep worsens. Their sleep worsens. They take more sleeping tablets. And so it goes.

This is a case where the way to get a better night's sleep is to stop taking sleeping tablets. You'll sleep worse for a few nights — everybody does when they stop the tablets — but then you'll settle back into a better night's sleep.

Of course, other drugs can make you snore. People who are still breathing after an overdose of heroin tend to snore. And snoring is more common in people with high blood pressure who take drugs like beta-blockers or methyldopa.

HOW LOUD CAN SNORING GET?

Snoring can get so loud that there is nothing in the world that you can imagine being louder. Snores have been measured at more than 90 decibels, which is as loud as a dog barking or a motorbike starting.

THE WORLD'S LOUDEST SNORER

Kare Walkert, a 44-year-old man of Kumla, Sweden, is honoured by the *Guinness Book of Records* as having the world's loudest snore. He was recorded reaching 93 decibels while sleeping at Orebro Regional Hospital in Sweden in 1993.

But even the quiet ones can drive you mad. It's not just the noise, it's the fact that the noise shouldn't be there. Mosquitoes are quiet, but they annoy because you know there just shouldn't be a hum in your ear when you are trying to get to sleep. In the same way, even a soft snore can keep the partner awake.

"His snore is louder than his war-cry."

Marcus Cato in *Plutarch's Lives: Marcus Cato*.
Written in the first century AD.

IF I'M SNORING SO LOUDLY, WHY DON'T I WAKE MYSELF UP?

There's no good explanation for this. Why is it that someone who snores so loudly that no one else can sleep in the same room can sleep through their own racket?

Do they actually wake themselves up, but so briefly, that they do not remember?

Have they damaged their own hearing that much that they have become near-deaf?

Or do they have domestic deafness? This is a cousin to domestic blindness, in which men can't see the butter in the fridge and have to call for help. And a second cousin to domestic stupidity, in which men who have lived in a house for 20 years still don't know where the vacuum cleaner is kept.

Or is it just that they have become used to it, in the same way that people living near an airport soon stop hearing the planes that drive visitors mad?

"There ain't no why to find out why a snorer can't hear himself snore."

Mark Twain in *Tom Sawyer Abroad.*

WHY DO BABIES SNORE?

Some newborn babies have obstructive sleep apnoea. They snore, they have noisy breathing and they often sweat while asleep. While awake, they may hold their breath at times, and while feeding they may have difficulty breathing and swallowing. They put on weight slowly, they grow slowly and they tend to have recurrent ear infections.

Studies have shown that these babies put their tongues back, blocking their airways temporarily, causing them to choke. This tends to happen during REM sleep, although it can happen at any time.

Obstructive sleep apnoea is more common in premature babies than those born at full term. It is also more common in boys than in girls, and in fat babies than thin babies. It becomes less common in all babies as they grow.

Some of these babies have anatomical problems in their mouth and pharynx. A few have genetic problems such as hypothyroidism or Down syndrome. On top of these underlying factors, infections causing increased secretions may be a factor.

There is some evidence that snoring and obstructive sleep apnoea may be linked to SIDS, or sudden infant death syndrome. But this research is in the fairly early stages, and it is too soon to be sure.

WHY DO OLDER CHILDREN SNORE?

Something like 10 per cent of children snore. Some children who snore have swollen adenoids, which are collections of lymph tissue (like glands) at the back of the nose in the upper part of the pharynx. Others have enlarged tonsils. In a few others, it's because of the shape of their face or their nose.

Twenty years ago, doctors were quick to whip out tonsils and adenoids because of recurrent infections. Around that time it was realised that many of these operations were not necessary, as the children would grow out of the infections. As well, every now and then a child dies after a tonsillectomy.

So tonsillectomy and adenoidectomy fell right out of favour. But they do have a role to play in the treatment of children who snore. There is now some concern that children who eventually have their tonsils and adenoids out for snoring have to be put through years of extensive testing and investigations. For example, in Israel over a 10-year period the average age of children having their adenoids out rose from 4 $\frac{1}{2}$ to almost eight. It makes you wonder how many operations are being unnecessarily delayed.

IS SNORING DANGEROUS IN CHILDREN?

That's a loaded question, partly because there hasn't been enough research done to answer it properly. But the most likely scenario is this.

Most children who snore do so because they have chronically enlarged tonsils or adenoids, and as long as the snoring is mild and they don't stop breathing then it is not doing them any harm.

But some children who snore — who knows what proportion — will probably find that it is doing them some harm, even if they don't know it.

Various studies of snoring in children have found the following things.

As with adults, children who snore sleep badly at night, are sleepy during the day and have difficulties concentrating. Some of them are hyperactive and have short attention spans. Some behave badly and perform poorly at school. Some wet their beds and have nightmares.

The only known study that looked at the effects of snoring on children's hearts found no impact on the heart's rhythm. That does not mean snoring does not cause heart disease — the study did not look down the track.

The main treatment for children who snore is removal of the tonsils and adenoids. In the right cases, this can cure the problem in an instant. But if the tonsils were not the cause, the procedure makes no difference apart from exposing the child to an unnecessary operation.

WHAT IS
SNORING DISEASE?

Snoring disease is an infection in birds such as the black-headed gull (Larus ridibundus Larus), which is found in Czechoslovakia and other parts of central Europe. It is caused by the protozoa Cryptosporidium, which infects the sinuses, pharynx, trachea and bronchi. When black-headed gull chicks are infected, they start snoring within a few days, and die a few days later.

It has nothing at all to do with humans, but I found it in a library and it seemed too good to ignore. Fascinating, isn't it?

yawn

"Snoring is a disease of listeners."

T. Macnab, A. Blokmanis and R.I. Dickson
of the University of British Columbia, Vancouver.

DOES SNORING
RUN IN FAMILIES?

To some extent, snoring does run in families. But nobody yet knows why.

Is there a snoring gene hidden away on the Y chromosome so that it affects only men? Will it be discovered one day so that snoring can be wiped off the face of the earth?

Or it is that the tendency to eat too much, drink too much and put on weight runs in families?

Or it is that the shape of your neck and the way you sleep at night with your head curled forward on your chest runs in families?

Or is it that people with narrow airways are born to parents with narrow airways, and have children with narrow airways.

The last explanation is the most likely, while the others may play a part.

CAN SNORING
HARM MY PARTNER?

Let me count the ways.

1. Snoring is incredibly, remarkably, unbelievably, horrendously annoying, unless you're the person doing it.

2. Snoring can harm the snoree, if that's the right way to describe someone who is snored upon, because it's so loud. Any chronic loud noise can harm the ears of the listener.

3. Some snorers often twitch and kick and punch and jerk in their sleep, so the snoree may well wake up sore.

My family has a traditional way of dealing with snorers. The woken woman reaches down into the bed and gives the penis of the snorer a tweak. Understandably, the snorer jumps and rolls onto his side to get away from the tweaker. Silence returns, until the next time the snorer rolls onto his back. That method seems to be effective, if not a little too bruising for comfort.

CASE STUDY

A 46-year-old woman went to her doctor in Salt Lake City, USA, because she couldn't keep any food or drink down. It sounded like there was something stuck low down in her oesophagus. Her doctor put a tube down to have a look, and found an earplug.

It turns out that the woman had married recently, and couldn't get used to her husband's snoring. So she wore earplugs. How she came to eat one, nobody knows.

---

4. The snoree may end up as sleep-deprived as you because of all the noise you are making.

5. The snoree may well end up sex-starved, too, as one of you moves into another room.

6. The snoree may become very tense as he or she listens to you choke and stop breathing each night.

WHAT'S THE CONNECTION BETWEEN SNORING AND EPILEPSY?

Doctors in an American hospital noticed that some of their patients with fairly severe epilepsy snored loudly. These same people were quite sleepy during the day and some were obese. They wondered.

They looked into it, and found that a few had sleep apnoea. After treatment with CPAP (continuous positive airway pressure see p. 88) or drugs, most felt better and they stopped having so many fits.

The doctors think that the sleep apnoea was reducing the flow of blood to the brain, which was reducing the amount of oxygen getting to the brain. This was making their brains more irritable and more likely to go into a seizure. Getting rid of the snoring helped their epilepsy.

This does not mean snoring causes epilepsy, just that in some people it might make it worse.

CAN SNORING BE
A SIGN OF OTHER
MEDICAL CONDITIONS?

Not really, but snoring and sleep disorders are common in people with certain other medical conditions. These include people with:

- sickle cell anaemia, in which the red blood cells, which carry oxygen, become deformed when oxygen levels drop

- Marfan's syndrome, in which the connective tissues (those that aren't bones or organs) are abnormal and the airways are narrow

---

A 48-year-old Japanese woman with multiple sclerosis suddenly developed the hiccups, and couldn't stop. They were so severe that after three weeks she had to be admitted to hospital. Tests showed that the multiple sclerosis had affected a small part of the brainstem. Treatment with high doses of steroids reduced the swelling in that area, and the hiccups stopped. She went home.

But her family brought her back to the hospital next day, because she was snoring so loudly they couldn't sleep. This eventually settled down with another drug, but again it shows that damage to the brain can make you snore.

A 53-year-old man went to the University of Bologna Medical School for a common problem — he was having trouble sleeping. But as the doctors there soon found out, his was no common case.

Until a couple of months earlier, he had been sleeping five to seven hours a night, with a 30-minute siesta in the afternoon. Soon he was down to two or three hours a night and no siesta. Worse still, he became impotent and lost his libido. A month later he was constipated, had a temperature and would sweat whenever he stood up.

Two months later he was down to the odd hour here and there, and what an odd hour it was. While asleep he would stand in his bed and give a military salute. He told relatives he was dreaming of a coronation.

He soon lost the ability to sleep at all and became exhausted. Then he became clumsy. Then drowsy. Over the next month he became confused, slipped into a coma and died, just nine months after the first problems appeared. His father, two sisters and at least a dozen other relatives, including a 20-year-old cousin, had all died the same way.

An autopsy found that the thalamus, a central part of the brain which controls the sleep-wake cycle, had degenerated. First he couldn't stay asleep, then he couldn't stay awake.

This is now recognised as fatal familial insomnia, an inherited disease which affects about 100 families around the world. There is no effective treatment.

- quadriplegia, in which the respiratory muscles are weak and breathing, even during the daytime, can be quite difficult

- hypothyroidism (low thyroid function), in which excess fat is deposited around the neck, making obstruction more likely, and in which the muscles of the neck don't work as well as they should

- acromegaly (gigantism), in which the tongue and other soft tissues of the pharynx grow larger, and in which the brain's drive to breathe is somehow disturbed

- polio, in which the muscles of the chest and pahrynx may have been weakened, making breathing at night difficult

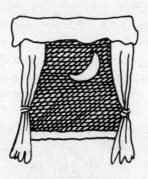

CAN I STILL HAVE SEX
AND SNORE?

Not at the same time, you can't. Well, you can if you follow the line, "Wake me up when you're finished".

Lots of people who snore heavily and who have obstructive sleep apnoea lose their sex drive. You can imagine the scene. You're tired, you have trouble concentrating, you're constantly falling asleep on the job, you have headaches, you have high blood pressure and a dicky heart. Sex is not always the most attractive proposition.

Look at it from your partner's point of view, too. You're tired, you have trouble concentrating, you're constantly falling asleep on the job, you have headaches, high blood pressure and a dicky heart. Sex is not always the most attractive proposition either.

On top of that, maybe you're overweight and you might drink and smoke too much. You snore, too. Loudly. You may even be wearing a CPAP (see p. 88) mask or a nasal dilator.

A guaranteed turn-on? Maybe not.

SHOULD I TAKE MY SNORING SERIOUSLY?

Yes. Look at all the problems that can occur. You, the person who may or may not have these problems, are not exactly the best person to judge whether you are affected.

For a start, you don't even know if you snore. You don't know how loud you snore. How often you snore. How annoyingly you snore.

You may realise you're tired during the day, but you may not be aware how often you're dropping off for a 10-second nap. You may not realise that your attention span has diminished and that your memory is going. How can you remember what your memory was like?

You may not be in the best position to judge whether you are drinking too much, or whether you should give up smoking. Most people are not all that rational about their smoking and drinking habits.

And you certainly would find it hard to tell whether your blood pressure was OK and your heart was in good nick. That, again, is something that only somebody else can judge.

DO I NEED TO SEE MY DOCTOR ABOUT MY SNORING?

It would be a good idea to see your family doctor if you snore regularly. For all the reasons covered in the previous pages, snoring may be dangerous for you. Of course, it doesn't have to be — many people snore every night and have no troubles from it.

But on the whole, snoring regularly increases your risk of heart attack, stroke, car accidents, dozing off during your favourite TV show and being kicked out of bed into the spare room.

It seems worth the effort to have a chat to your doctor about your snoring. In some cases, the GP will recommend formal sleep studies to see whether the problem is serious and requires medical treatment. In other cases, the doctor will recommend losing weight, slowing down the drinking and giving up the smokes.

But it's hard for you to tell which category you fall

"The nurse sleeps sweetly, hir'd to watch the sick, whom snoring she disturbs."

William Cowper in *The Task*, 1785.

into. There is no one single question, or even combination of questions, that you can ask yourself to decide whether your snoring is doing you harm or not. Your doctor will have a better chance of working it out.

There is one tool that you can use to work out how sleepy you are during the day. It's called the Epworth Sleepiness Scale, and was developed by Dr Murray Johns of the sleep disorders unit at the Epworth Hospital in Melbourne.

On the next page is a copy of the questionnaire. Dr Johns says the normal range of scores is 0–10. If you are scoring above 10, you may be running into trouble.

THE EPWORTH
SLEEPINESS SCALE

How likely are you to doze off or fall asleep in the following situations, in contrast to just feeling tired? This refers to your usual way of life in recent times.

Even if you haven't done some of these things recently, try to work out how they would have affected you.

Use the following scale to choose the *most appropriate number* for each situation:

0   would *never* doze
1   *slight* chance of dozing
2   *moderate* chance of dozing
3   *high* chance of dozing

"Laugh and the world laughs with you; snore and you sleep alone."

ascribed to both American poet Ella Wheeler Wilcox
and to British novelist Anthony Burgess.

Situation	Chance of dozing
Sitting and reading	. . . .
Watching TV	. . . .
Sitting inactive in a public place (eg. a theatre or a meeting)	. . . .
As a passenger in a car for an hour without a break	. . . .
Lying down to rest in the afternoon when circumstances permit	. . . .
Sitting and talking to someone	. . . .
Sitting quietly after a lunch without alcohol	. . . .
In a car while stopped for a few minutes in the traffic	. . . .
Total	. . . .

Source: Dr Murray Johns

If you snore and choke at night and your score is higher than 10, then you have a high chance of having significant sleep apnoea, which may be associated with all the problems mentioned in the rest of the book. If you have a low score, and do not choke at night, then serious problems caused by your snoring are unlikely.

Dealing with Snoring

73

HOW DO I KNOW IF IT IS SERIOUS?

As I said before, it is very hard to know whether your snoring is just snoring, or whether it can be causing you serious problems. Signs that your snoring is probably serious include:

- if you are sleepy during the day;

- if your snoring is intermittent during the night;

- if you partner says you stop breathing during the night;

- if you kick your legs or wave your arms around while snoring;

- if your snoring has changed its character or volume recently.

But it may be possible to have problems caused by snoring without any of these signs.

TESTS FOR SNORING

Before you can work out what to do about snoring, it may be wise to work out what is making you snore. This requires a few tests.

Physical examination

Your doctor should give you a thorough physical examination if you snore. That should include a check on your height, weight, pulse, blood pressure and an examination of your chest, heart, nose, throat and nervous system.

The doctor should also talk to the person you sleep with (or the one who has kicked you out into another room, but who you would like to sleep with again). It is impossible for you to describe what you do while you're asleep, so make sure your bed partner (or partners, if you so choose) go along with you.

Blood tests

You may have some blood tests to help investigate your snoring.

Full blood count Among other things, this test checks the amount of haemoglobin, which carries oxygen, and the number of red blood cells, which carry haemoglobin.

If you have too little haemoglobin, you are anaemic. This will make you tired, and may make much worse any problems that snoring or sleep apnoea is giving you.

Some people with severe sleep apnoea develop a condition known as polycythaemia, which means they have too many red blood cells. These form in response to the lack of oxygen in their bloodstream. It is a condition which can cause problems in the long term, although treatment of the sleep apnoea should get rid of the polycythaemia.

Thyroid function tests If your thyroid gland is not working properly, then you may lay down extra deposits of fat in your neck, making snoring more likely. See page 24 & 65 for more details.

Sleep studies

Sleep studies take place in a dedicated sleep centre, although within a few years, sleep studies will probably be done in your home using portable equipment. You stay overnight, usually just for one night, and have the terribly difficult job of going to sleep.

Before you go to bed, you will be hooked up to various monitors which will measure your brain activity, heart rate and blood oxygen levels during the night. An EEG (electroencephalograph — which is an instrument used for recording electrical activity of the brain) will define the stages of sleep as will monitors attached to your eyes and chin. The heart rate monitor

"Snoring: to sleep out loud."

Anon.

will tell whether your heart rate slows when you snore. The blood oxygen measurement is to find out whether the amount of oxygen drops when you snore, and how much it drops if you stop breathing. You will also have monitors attached to your chest and abdomen to measure the movement of your diaphragm.

With sleep studies and the other investigations, your doctor should be able to advise on the cause of your snoring, the extent to which it may be causing you problems and the most effective solution or solutions.

LIFESTYLE CHANGES

Almost everybody who snores would benefit from some changes in lifestyle. The general advice is to:

- lose weight

- get some regular exercise

- cut back the drink

- give up the smokes

- avoid sleeping tablets and other drugs.

Lose weight

Most people think that to lose weight they have to go on a diet. That is not true. You lose weight not by going on a diet — diets rarely work for more than a couple of months — but by changing your eating habits and getting some regular exercise.

Many diets that people sell to you or that are published in magazines are complicated. There are charts to follow. They tell you to weigh food. They get you to count calories. It's all a load of rubbish.

The simplest thing to remember is this. Excess weight is stored energy. If you're overweight, then you can consider yourself a bundle of energy. Your task is to free it.

Food is energy. Exercise releases energy. To rid your body of that excess energy, you need to release more from exercise than you consume from eating. Simple. A no-fuss approach to all this is as follows:

- eat breakfast

- don't eat morning tea

- eat lunch

- don't eat afternoon tea

- eat dinner

- don't eat supper

- don't have takeaways any more than once a week

- get some exercise.

While you're deciding when to eat (and the answer is three times a day), you also need to decide what to eat. Again, the simplest approach is likely to be the best. You should eat foods that you enjoy which you feel may be healthy, and avoid too many foods which you suspect may be fattening. Most people know in their hearts which foods are fattening and which are not — it's sometimes just a matter of listening to your heart.

To help, here's some basic information adapted from the Australian Nutrition Foundation.

Eat a lot of:
- grain products like breads, cereals, rice, spaghetti and oatmeal;
- fruit;
- vegetables.

Eat moderate amounts of:
- meats;
- dairy products.

Eat little:
- butter, margarine and oils
- added salt
- sugar.

The importance of following this sort of approach, rather than eating little packets of something from a weight-loss centre, is this. Nobody can afford to belong to a weight-loss centre for the rest of their life. Yet you will have to maintain whatever weight loss you have achieved for the rest of your life. So it's no good starving yourself for three months, then find the weight gets piled back on.

You have to change the pattern of the way you eat, but you have to find a comfortable way of doing it. The changes you are to make should be ones you will make for life. For example, if you hate grapefruit don't say you'll eat it for breakfast every day.

Get some regular exercise

You don't need to join a gym or run 10km a day to get some exercise. The amount of exercise that will improve your heart and help you lose weight is surprisingly little.

Purely on the heart, there is good evidence that people who exercise regularly are only half as likely as slobs to get heart disease. Exercise reduces the amount of fat in your blood, and makes you less likely to develop diabetes and osteoporosis. Exercise also lowers your blood pressure.

Researchers have shown that you don't need to join a gym to lower your blood pressure. All that is needed is regular exercise as little as three times a week. Once you start regular exercise, your blood pressure drops almost immediately. Maintaining the exercise maintains the lowered blood pressure, although it shoots back up within three weeks of you stopping. There is almost no difference in exercising three times or seven times a week.

What sort of exercise is best? Moderate exercise — say cycling until you work up a mild sweat for 30 minutes — three times a week reduces blood pressure, as does walking five times a week, although to a lesser

"Sound peoples sleep is not alike, some snoar in their sleep, others without a noise."

A Fox in *Wurtz' Surgery*, 1658.

extent. Swimming also works. But high intensity, short duration exercise — such as sprints or games of squash — have no effect on blood pressure.

An important feature of this research into exercise is that it proves it is never too late to start. The biggest jump in the death rate is between people who do absolutely nothing and those who do the bare minimum. Even a walk around the block three evenings a week saves lives. All you need is your feet and a road.

To make it easy on yourself, set aside a regular time each day. When you wake up, or at lunchtime, or after dinner.

Find yourself a walking partner. Your partner. Your neighbour. Your son or daughter. A friend from work. If you are doing it with somebody, then on the days you don't feel so keen, your walking partner will spur you on.

If you can find somewhere pretty like a park or a creek, then that's good. But if not, then walk around the block. Say hello to your neighbours. Watch their gardens grow. Get to know their children. Get some fresh air.

Regular exercise will do three main things. It will help cut down any stresses in your life. It will help you lose weight, so it will reduce the snoring and whatever problems go with it. And it will help you live longer.

*"Thou do'st snore distinctly
There's meaning in thy snores."*

Sebastian in Shakepeare's *The Tempest.*

Cut back the drink

For all the reasons outlined on pages 27 & 28, alcohol and snoring do not mix. You might find that cutting back on the drinking after dinner, or having your two drinks before dinner instead of after, is enough to do the trick. Or if you are a heavy drinker, you may feel you need to cut right back.

For your health generally, the National Health and Medical Research Council recommends that:

- men have no more than 28 standard drinks a week, and have at least two alcohol-free days each week; and

- women have no more than 14 standard drinks a week, and have at least two alcohol-free days each week.

If alcohol is giving you a specific problem, such as sleep apnoea, then a reduction below those recommended maximums may be necessary.

Apart from helping your muscles stay firmer, the other advantage of cutting back the drink is that you will lose weight. That, too, will help.

Give up the smokes

If you smoke, giving up will do you the world of good. You'll be able to walk further, talk easier, move faster and you will probably live longer. Within a couple of years, your risk of having a heart attack and of developing the many cancers caused by smoking should have almost returned to normal. And your snoring may ease up.

There are many ways to give up smoking. You can go to specialised Quit programs. You can try counsellors and hypnotists. You can attend clinics. You can buy nicotine replacement gums and patches. They all work to varying degrees.

Or you can just stop. Most people in Australia who have given up smoking, and there are several million of them around, have done it on their own. They have decided to quit and have done so. It may have taken them two or three, or five or six goes. And they will not have enjoyed it. But they have done it.

Avoid sleeping tablets and other drugs

Many people have become used to taking sleeping tablets every night. The odd thing is that sleeping tablets do not work very well after the first two weeks

In Greek mythology, Sleep is the son of Night and the brother of Death.

The trouble is that when you try to come off them, it can be hard to sleep at first.

Most sleeping tablets destroy REM sleep, which is the main time in which we dream. After a couple of weeks, they lose their effect on general sleep, but they still keep down the amount of REM sleep we have.

If, after a month, you want to come off sleeping tablets, you develop what is known as REM rebound. You get twice as much REM sleep in the night as you would normally have, and it's all full of dreams. You have so many dreams that you think you can't possibly have had a good night's sleep.

If you don't use sleeping tablets, good. They are OK for the odd night, but they are a bad habit to form.

If you use sleeping tablets regularly and have done so for a while, it would be wise to wean yourself off them. Use a slightly smaller dose each night and gradually rely on them less. Then be prepared for a week or so of unsettled sleep when you finally stop them.

Sleep experts recommend that most people can sleep well without tablets if they develop what is known as good sleep hygiene. Sleep hygiene is basically a routine that says you do much the same thing each night and use your bed only for sleep or sex.

Following are a few tips on good sleep hygiene:

- get up at the same time each day

- have a quiet time before bed each night

- develop a bedtime routine — go to the toilet, clean your teeth, have a drink of water then get into bed

- don't read in bed

- don't watch television in bed

- if you can't sleep, get up and read for 30 minutes in another room, they try again

Some sleep experts suggest you should go to bed at the same time each night, although others say you should only go to bed when you are tired enough to sleep.

COFFEE, TEA AND SOFT DRINKS

It sounds odd, but coffee, tea and soft drinks may help lighten your snoring. Most people snore more loudly when deeply asleep. The caffeine in coffee, tea and soft drinks will probably lighten your sleep, which may lighten your snoring.

WHEN DOCTORS ARE NEEDED

I f you have obstructive sleep apnoea that is either quite severe or persists despite you making the recommended lifestyle changes, you may need more help. The main forms of medical treatment are:

- continuous positive airway pressure (CPAP)

- surgery

- devices such as Nozovent

CPAP

CPAP is continuous positive airway pressure, and it was invented in the early 1980s by Professor Colin Sullivan and colleagues at the Royal Prince Alfred Hospital in Sydney. Used in the right people, it is a highly effective treatment to reduce snoring and reduce the complications of obstructive sleep apnoea. But it is not a treatment that should be used lightly, as it can be quite disruptive. And it should not be considered a cure — it is a treatment that should be used every night, and the problems return if it is not used.

What does it look like?

CPAP comprises a mask which you wear on your face and a pump to drive air into the mask. The mask fits tightly over your nose and is held on by straps running over the top of your head and under your ears.

Coming from the mask is a piece of tubing which runs to the pump. The pump is powered by electricity.

If you use CPAP, you might feel a bit like a space cadet. It can take a bit of getting used to. But about 70 per cent of people who start using CPAP wear it regularly, so it must be reasonably comfortable.

How does it work?

The idea of CPAP is that it continually pumps air into your mouth and pharynx under pressure. That pressure, which is adjustable, keeps the pharynx open and stops the flutter of the uvula, soft palate and whatever else is waving in the breeze.

If the airway is open, there should be no snoring. There should be no drop in oxygen levels. There should be no rise in blood pressure nor strain on the heart. There should be no interruption to sleep and no sleepiness next day. There should be a return of normal memory and concentration. That's what should happen.

What effect does it have?

Most people who have CPAP feel better within a few days of using it. Most of those things described above that should happen do happen.

Some people report that they are doing better at work, that they are feeling like taking up sport and exercise again, and that they generally have much more energy than previously.

As well, wives and husbands of snorers usually say they are sleeping better, because the noise of the pump is easier to ignore than the noise of the snorer.

What problems does it cause?

The most common problems caused by CPAP, and what you can do about them, are:

- runny nose — this usually starts up soon after you start using the machine, and often goes away within a few weeks (although it can persist). Warming the bedroom, warming the tube by running it under the bedclothes or using a vaporiser to increase the humidity can all help;

- dry nose — rub vaseline into the inside of both nostrils;

- mask problems — the mask may not fit properly or may can soreness where it lies on the face. If this happens, adjust the straps to ensure a snug fit and rub a cream such as vitamin E into the face regularly;

- a noisy pump — you can get extra long tubing and leave the pump outside your bedroom.

It is important to remember that although CPAP helps, it doesn't cure the problem. As soon as you come off CPAP, the snoring returns and all the complications can reappear.

Are people saying they feel better just because they've had to go through the pain and disruption of an operation, so they are trying to justify their decision to themselves? Or is it that doctors aren't very good at measuring subtle improvements? Or is it that it works reasonably for snoring, but not for sleep apnoea? Does it get rid of the loose tissues that cause the noise of snoring, but do nothing for the underlying obstruction that causes apnoea?

UPPP has a number of possible side-effects. Many people find their voice becomes more nasal, and some experience sudden choking sensations while eating. Occasionally, someone's snoring becomes worse because of scarring in the throat after the operation.

UPPP has one big advantage as a treatment for someone with heavy snoring but not obstructive sleep apnoea. If it works, and there is no guarantee of that, it is a one-off treatment. CPAP and drug treatments are probably for life.

BULLDOGS

UPPP was first developed in Japan in the 1950s as a treatment for heavy snoring, then for many years it was used mainly by vets treating bulldogs, who have short fats necks and difficulty breathing.

It hit the Western world in 1981 and was taken up enthusiastically. Some of that first flush of enthusiasm has faded, but the operation is still used fairly widely.

PPGP

PPGP involves surgical removal of part of the palate, part of the pharynx and part of the tongue.

PPGP is a relatively new operation, and as yet it is impossible to talk about long-term results. However, the surgeons who have performed the operations believe it has helped a significant proportion of their patients, although it is not a cure.

If this operation is suggested, you should talk to your surgeon about risks and expected benefits.

Laser palatoplasty

Laser palatoplasty is slightly different from the other forms of surgery. Rather than cutting tissue off the soft palate, it uses a laser to scar the palate. This stiffens it, which stops it flapping about in the breeze so much.

It appears to have fewer side-effects than other forms of surgery, and you can be in and out of hospital in a day. There is little risk of bleeding after the operation.

While it sounds promising, laser palatoplasty is another form of surgery that has not been used often enough and for long enough to really find out whether or not it works.

Other surgery

Until UPPP came along, the main form of surgery for life-threatening obstructive sleep apnoea was a tracheotomy — a permanent hole in the trachea. It is a messy-looking operation with many complications, and is now restricted to patients who have severe complications from sleep apnoea and don't get better with other forms of treatment.

Some surgeons have tried operations to change the shape of the jaw in people whose obstruction rises from the structure of their bones. It may be able to help in the right people, although further work is needed to prove this.

NON-SURGICAL
NASAL TREATMENTS

A blocked nose does not necessarily require surgery. In fact, other forms of treatment that don't involve surgery should be used before surgery is contemplated.

Nasal sprays

If your nose is blocked regularly and you snore, it is worth trying to clear your nose with a decongestant spray. The most commonly used ones reduce the swelling and may make a difference, but will need to be used several times a day. Also, the sorts of sprays you can buy without prescription tend to cause a rebound effect when you stop using them.

More recently, other types of nasal sprays have been developed. They contain steroids, and aim to reduce the swelling in the long term and prevent it happening. These are effective treatments for hayfever and allergic rhinitis (an allergy-based runny nose), and can help some people who snore. They need to be used for several months to reach their full effect.

Nasal dilators

If you have a blocked nose, try this. Hold each nostril with your thumb and index finger and pull outwards. You may well find it easier to breathe through your nose. That is the principle behind nasal dilators — if they make it easier for you to breathe through your nose, you will snore less and are less likely to suffer from obstructive sleep apnoea.

The most commonly used nasal dilator is Nozovent, which is a device worn on the nose each night to keep the nostrils open.

Some snorers who try a Nozovent say they feel better after using it. They say they sleep better and have to breathe through their mouths less often. Some will snore less, although some will snore more as more air flows through the pharynx. Not all doctors are convinced Nozovent helps much, but some recommend it. It is certainly not as intrusive as surgery and CPAP, and it may be worth a try.

TENNIS BALLS

An old trick is to sew a tennis ball into the back of your pyjama top. Now try to sleep on your back. Not easy, is it?

Devices

There are a whole range of devices available which fit in the mouth at night. These are known generally as mandibular advancement devices, because they push the jaw, or mandible, forward. This helps to keep the tongue away from the throat and frees up the airway.

Some mandibular advancement devices have to be fitted by a dentist, while others can be fitted by a doctor. Some are said to be quite comfortable, while others are harder to get used to.

Mandibular advancement devices reduce snoring in about three-quarters of the people who use them, although they do little for people with sleep apnoea. It is impossible to know which people they will help, and which they will not.

Late last night I slew my wife,
Stretched her on the parquet flooring;
I was loth to take her life,
But I had to stop her snoring!

Harry Graham, "Necessity" in *Ruthless Rhymes*, 1899.

Drug treatments

Some doctors, although not a lot, use drug treatment for people with obstructive sleep apnoea. One drug is medroxyprogesterone, which is a form of the female hormone progesterone. It stimulates the drive to breathe. Another is protriptyline, which is a form of antidepressant.

Neither of these drugs have been shown to be all that effective, and both have side-effects worth watching out for. But if effective, they are less intrusive than CPAP and, in the right person, may be just as effective.

WHERE TO GET HELP

AUSTRALIAN
SLEEP CENTRES

NSW
Camperdown Sleep Disorders Centre
Concord Hospital
Hornsby Sleep Disorders Centre
Royal Newcastle Hospital
Royal North Shore Hospital
Royal Prince Alfred Hospital

Victoria
Epworth Hospital
Heidelberg Repatriation Hospital
Monash Medical Centre

Queensland
Greenslopes Repatriation Hospital
Mater Children's Hospital
Princess Alexandra Hospital
Prince Charles Hospital
Wesley Hospital

SA
Adelaide Children's Hospital
Daw Park Repatriation Hospital
Royal Adelaide Hospital
Queen Elizabeth Hospital

WA	Princess Margaret Hospital for Children
	Sir Charles Gairdner Hospital
ACT	Canberra Sleep Laboratory

NEW ZEALAND SLEEP CENTRE

Auckland	Respiratory Clinic,
	Greenlane Hospital

AUSTRALIAN PROFESSIONAL BODIES

Australasian Sleep Association
c/– Dr John Wheatley
Department of Respiratory Medicine
Westmead Hospital
Westmead NSW 2145
ph: (02) 845 6797

Thoracic Society of Australia and New Zealand
145 Macquarie St
Sydney NSW 2000
ph: (02) 256 5457

AUSTRALIAN SLEEP DISORDERS GROUPS

Sleep Apnoea Research Association (SARA)
PO Box 303
Roseville NSW 2069
ph: (02) 415 6300

Sleep Apnoea of Victoria Education and Research
Society (SAVERS)
PO Box 446
North Balwyn VIC 3104
ph: (03) 859 6101

Narcolepsy and Overwhelming Daytime Sleep Society
(NODSS)
PO Box 100
Rosanna VIC 3084
ph: (03) 435 4525

Australian Ventilator Users Network
PO Box 211
Fairfield VIC 3078
ph: (03) 481 1268 (have phone answering machine)

Sleep Apnoea Research Association (Qld)
PO Box 1182
Coorparoo DC Qld 4151
ph: (07) 801 1003

Adelaide Apnoea
49 Gunther Pde
Pasadina SA 5042
ph: (08) 374 1561 (have phone answering machine)

Sleep Apnoea Research Association (Canberra region)
PO Box 1461
Tuggeranong ACT 2901
ph: (06) 296 1889

Sleep Apnoea Support Group
11 Grandview Pl, Norwood
Launceston TAS 7250
ph: (003) 44 7261

By late 1996, a national association of sleep apnoea support groups should be formed. For details, please contact any of the above groups.

NEW ZEALAND SLEEP DISORDER GROUPS

Sleep Apnoea Association of N.Z. Inc. (SAANZ)
P.O. Box 24-527
Royal Oak, Auckand 3
ph/fax: (09) 625 6021

Sleep Aponea Patient Trust (SAPT)
c/- Mrs. P. Ritchie, Hon. Sec.,
P.O. Box 19-728, Christchurch
ph: (03) 381 0544

The Snoring Bedmate

You thunder at my side,
Lad of ceaseless hum;
There's not a saint would chide
My prayer that you were dumb.

The dead start from the tomb
With each blare from your nose.
I suffer, with less room,
Under these bedclothes.

Which could I better bide
Since my head's already broke —
Your pipe-drone at my side,
Woodpecker's drill on oak?

Brass scraped with knicky knives,
A cowbell's tinny clank,
Or the yells of tinker's wives
Giving birth behind a bank?

A drunken, braying clown
Slapping cards down on a board
Were less easy to disown
Than the softest snore you've snored.

Sweeter the grunts of swine
Than yours that win release.
Sweeter, bedmate mine,
The screech of grieving geese.

Silent Night

A sick calf's moan for aid,
A broken mill's mad clatter,
The snarl of flood cascade ...
Christ! Now what's the matter?

That was a ghastly growl!
What signified that twist? —
An old wolf's famished howl,
Wave-boom at some cliff's breast?

Storm screaming round a crag,
Bellow of raging bull,
Hoarse bell of rutting stag,
Compared with this were lull!

Ah, now a gentler fall —
Bark of crazy hound?
Brats squabbling for a ball?
Ducks squawking on a pond?

No, rougher weather's back again.
Some great ship's about to sink
And roaring bursts the main
Over the bulwark's brink!

Farewell, tonight, to sleep.
Every gust across the bed
Makes hair rise and poor flesh creep.
Would that one of us were dead!

This version by John V Kelleher in *The Faber Book of Irish Verse*, edited by
John Montague, published by Faber & Faber (London, 1974).